A European Foreign Policy?
Decision-Making in European
External Policy

Brendan Donnelly,
Stephen Haseler
& Jeannette Ladzik

Introduction

This is a study of the European Union's external decision-making processes and the present debate which surrounds them. It considers in turn three main elements of these processes, the Common Foreign and Security Policy (CFSP), the External Security and Defence Policy (ESDP) and the Common Commercial Policy (CCP). The opportunities and challenges for the European Union's position in the wider world are similar in each area, but each case study presents sufficient aspects peculiar to itself to justify separate treatment. In all three sections, a brief historical review will lead into a discussion of recent institutional and political developments. Inevitably, the work of the European Constitutional Convention, the Intergovernmental Conference which followed it and the new situation created by the French and Dutch referendums will be at the heart of this discussion. Our three principal topics have all figured prominently in this complex series of debates and events. The study will conclude with a series of recommendations arising in our view from the events and circumstances we describe. Between our consideration of recent developments and our recommendations is an analysis of the broader geo-political context against which our largely institutional discussion can best be understood. The study ends with a section of concluding reflections from the authors.

Brendan Donnelly, Stephen Haseler & Jeannette Ladzik

Common Foreign and Security Policy

Historical background

Until the Maastricht Treaty of 1992, the European Community's aspirations towards co-ordination in the making of foreign policy found expression in the framework of European Political Co-operation (EPC). This arrangement, initially based on the Davignon report of 1970 and later formalised in the Single European Act of 1987, facilitated the exchange of information and analysis between the EC's foreign ministries, and was intended to ensure that the foreign policies of the six (later twelve) member states of the Community should diverge as little as possible. The underlying goal of EPC was not the establishment of a single European foreign policy, but rather the greater co-ordination of the separate foreign policies adopted by the individual member states of the Community.

The historic events of 1989 to 1991 brought to the EC's member states a new interest in the possibility of a genuinely common European foreign policy. The end of the Cold War, the following period of uncertainty in Eastern Europe and increasing doubts about the USA's willingness to remain engaged in Europe, reinforced the willingness of most of the

Community's member states at least to discuss the establishment of structures for a common foreign and security policy. The European Council, meeting at Maastricht in December 1991, adopted the Maastricht Treaty, which among other provisions announced the replacement of European Political Cooperation by a 'Common Foreign and Security Policy' with the objectives of safeguarding 'the common values, fundamental interests and independence of the Union', of promoting 'international co-operation' and of developing and consolidating 'democracy and the rule of law, and respect of human rights and fundamental freedom' (Art.J.1).[1] The Treaty also envisaged the "eventual framing' of a common defence policy between the member states, which might "in time" lead to a common defence structure for Europe (Art.J.4).

While the decisions of the Maastricht European Council represented some advance on what had gone before, they were nevertheless a compromise among the competing visions and interests of the member states, and a disappointment for a number of participants. The Maastricht Treaty envisaged in the Common Foreign and Security Policy only a limited role for the European Commission and the European Parliament, while the European Court of Justice was excluded entirely. All specific issues of the CFSP were to be centred on the Council, more precisely in the General Affairs Council of the foreign ministers from the member states. The Council would decide by unanimity, with qualified majority voting only being used for implementing decisions flowing from previous policy agreements arrived at by unanimity or consensus. Significantly, even this last possibility has never been used in practice over the past fifteen years.

The Maastricht Treaty came into force in November 1993, but already the limitations of the Union's new CFSP were apparent. As Yugoslavia disintegrated into civil war, the EU was humiliatingly unable to bring peace to the warring factions. Both in the Balkans and in Washington, the EU was seen as weak and divided. This marginalisation of the Union in matters on its European doorstep acted in the medium term as a spur to further co-ordination. The Amsterdam Treaty of 1997 contained an important provision designed to make the EU's Common Foreign and Security Policy more coherent and effective.

The Amsterdam Treaty maintained the underlying inter-governmental and consensual nature of decision-making in the CFSP, but broke new ground in creating a High Representative for the Union's Common Foreign and Security Policy. Predictably, the powers of this Representative were a matter of great controversy in the negotiations preceding the Treaty. The Representative's remit was more limited than a number of member states would have wished. His or her function was simply to assist the Council, of which he became Secretary General, 'in matters coming within the scope of CFSP, in particular through contributing to the for-mulation, preparation and implementation of policy deci-sions, and, when appropriate and acting on behalf of the Council at the request of the Presidency, through conducting political dialogue with third countries' (Art.J.16).[2] The High Representative was the servant of the Council and of no other European institution. He or she could only represent to third parties policies and analyses adopted by unanimity within the Council. The first and so far only High Representative is the former Spanish Foreign Minister Javier Solana, who is widely regarded as having carried out his lim-ited remit with the greatest possible effectiveness that cir-cumstances allowed.

Even after the Maastricht, Amsterdam and Nice Treaties, most member states still believed that the EU's performance in its Common Foreign and Security Policy fell far short of expectations, given the Union's potential economic and diplomatic weight in the world. It was in the light of such concerns that the European Council of Laeken in 2001 asked the "Convention on the Future of Europe" to consider how to improve the instruments of the EU's external action so that the EU can become 'a power [...] to change the course of the world'. The Convention should particularly consider the problems of "coherence, effectiveness and legitimacy." The response of the Convention to this challenge was to propose a new system for the external representation and internal development of the Union's CFSP, centred on the creation of an EU Foreign Minister and the setting up of an "External Action Service." These proposals were subsequently incorporated into the Constitutional Treaty, but their future implementation has been rendered uncertain by the stalemate over the Treaty's own ratification.

The European Foreign Minister

From the beginning of the Convention's work, it was common ground that the role and competences of the High Representative needed to be reviewed. Some participants in the Convention favoured retention of the Representative's present remit, perhaps with greater administrative resources for its execution. Others favoured a merging of the role of Representative with that of the European Commissioner for External Affairs. Others, while favouring a remodelling of the Representative's role, believed that confusion and conflicts of interest would be the outcome of any such merger. The Convention's working group on "External Action" reflected these differences of view in the four proposals which it presented to the Convention in December, 2002, and which formed the basis of the Convention's subsequent discussion of these issues. These options were essentially the maintenance of the High Representative's present functions; the incorporation of the High Representative into the European Commission; the merger of the post of High Representative and Commissioner for External Affairs, with the individual concerned answering to both the Council and the Commission; and the merger of the two posts, with the individual concerned reporting exclusively to the Council.[3]

Before the Convention members as a whole began to consider the report of the working group on 'External Action', the French and German governments submitted a paper to the Convention arguing for the creation of a European Foreign Minister, who should be at the same time a member of the Commission and also a servant of the Council of Ministers, essentially the third option of the working group.[4] This 'double-hatting' concept was met with scepticism among some Convention members, albeit for different reasons. Whereas the federalist camp feared the collegiality of the Commission could be put in jeopardy by this concept, Peter Hain, belonging to the intergovernmental camp, regarded the "double-hatting" as unhelpful for reducing tensions between the Commission, the Council and the member states. His recipe for clarity was the unique subordination of the Representative/Foreign Minister to the Council.

In the event, both the Convention and the following Intergovernmental Conference adopted essentially the Franco-German proposals for a European Foreign Minister with reporting and other responsibilities to both the Council and the Commission. In agreeing to set up this new post, the member states, however, were careful to preserve their own position. In Article.I-28.4 of the Constitutional Treaty it is stipulated that in exercising his responsibilities within the Commission, the Union's Foreign Minister 'shall be bound by Commission procedures to the extent that it is consistent with paragraphs 2 and 3'.[5] Since paragraphs 2 and 3 set out the Foreign Minister's responsibilities to the Council, the potential effect of this Article is to subordinate the Minister's activities within the Commission to his responsibilities vis-à-vis the Council.

This desire of the majority of member states to stress their predominant role in supervising the Foreign Minister is further illustrated by the appointment and resignation procedures for the Minister. According to the Constitutional Treaty, the European Foreign Minister is to be appointed by the European Council, acting by qualified majority, requiring only the agreement of the President of the Commission (Art.I-28). The Minister's appointment as one of the Vice-Presidents of the Commission would need beyond the above described process the approval of the European Parliament, since the College of Commissioners must be endorsed as a whole by the European Parliament (Art.I-27.2). However, in contrast to the other Commissioners, the Minister would be spared the individual parliamentary ratification hearings. To end the Minister's term the same procedure as for the appointment applies, namely that the European Council would be entitled to dismiss the European Foreign Minister after having obtained agreement by the President of the Commission (Art.I-28.1). The Minister must also resign following a personal request by the President of the Commission, although even in this case the European Council must endorse the President's request. If the European Parliament votes on a censure motion on the Commission, 'the members of the Commission shall resign as a body and the Union Minister for Foreign Affairs shall resign from the duties that he or she carries out in the Commission' (Art.I-26.8).[6]

The European Foreign Minister's powers
The functions of the European Foreign Minister, as granted by the Constitutional Treaty, are essentially five-fold: initiative, co-ordination, representation, implementation, and crisis management.[7]

Initiative
With regard to the Minister's rights of initiative, 'he or she shall contribute by his or her proposals to the development' of the CFSP' (Art.I-28.2). The European Foreign Minister may collaborate with the Commission to submit in the area of CFSP joint proposals to the Council (Art.III-293.2). The Foreign Minister may also 'refer any question relating to the

common foreign and security policy to the Council' and may 'submit to it initiatives or proposals as appropriate'. This arrangement would represent a distinct promotion for the Minister and a demotion for the Commission, which until the Constitutional Treaty was able to table initiatives for CFSP policies. Specific rights of initiative accorded the Minister include that for the application of qualified majority voting in CFSP, a process which the Minister can invoke 'following a specific request to him or her from the European Council'.

Co-ordination
Among the range of co-ordination rights attributed to the European Foreign Minister, the most visible is the Presidency of the Foreign Affairs Council and the chairmanship of Political and Security Committee meetings. These functions have been exercised (and are still being exercised) by representatives of the national government holding the rotating Presidency of the Union. More generally, the Constitutional Treaty stipulates that as one of the Vice-Presidents of the Commission, the European Foreign Minister 'shall [also] ensure the consistency of the Union's external action, ' bringing together all the various aspects of the Union's policies in the wider world. The Minister should also 'be responsible within the Commission for responsibilities incumbent on it in external relations..."(Art.I-28.4). In addition to his own responsibilities, therefore, the Minister has a co-ordinating role towards his colleagues in the Commission who exercise responsibilities in the other policy fields relating to external actions. Finally, the Minister is enjoined to ensure that 'member states [...] support the common foreign and security policy actively and unreservedly in a spirit of loyalty and mutual solidarity' (Art.III-294.2). In theory this is a substantial task given to the Minister. In reality, the Minister has no formal sanction which he can apply against recalcitrant member states.

Representation

Since one major objective underlying the creation of the European Foreign Minister post was the improvement of the EU's ability to speak and act in a more unified manner on the international scene, the Constitutional Treaty provided the Minister with important representative functions. According to Art.III-296.2, which builds on the mandate already given to the High Representative (see Chapter1), the Union's Minister 'shall represent the Union for matters relating to the common foreign and security policy'. Art.III-305.1 charges the Minister to organise and co-ordinate member states' action in international organisations and at international conferences. When the EU had defined its position on a subject discussed at the UN Security Council 'those Member States which sit on the Security Council shall request that the Union Minister for Foreign Affairs be asked to present the Union's position'. How far and how often France and Britain would ever be willing to observe the letter and spirit of this article can only be a matter for speculation. The representational functions of the Minister are limited by Art.I-22.2 of the Constitutional Treaty, which allows the new President of the European Council as well to represent the EU to the outside world 'on issues concerning its common foreign and security policy'. Although the provision is included in the Treaty that this should happen 'without prejudice to the powers of the Union Minister for Foreign Affairs', the scope for conflicting claims of competence between the Minister and the President is clear. Similar conflicts might arise between the Minister and the Commission, which would retain its function under the Constitutional Treaty of external representation for the EU 'with the exception of the common foreign and security policy.' (Art.I-26.1).

Implementation

Art.I-40.4 provides that CFSP 'shall be put into effect by the Union Minister of Foreign Affairs and by the Member States'

Brendan Donnelly, Stephen Haseler & Jeannette Ladzik

while Art.III-296.1 says more precisely that the Minister 'shall ensure implementation of the European decisions adopted by the European Council and the Council of Ministers'.

Crisis Management
When crisis management is at issue, the Minister is given a particularly important role by the Constitutional Treaty. He would have the authority to propose the initiation of a military or civil mission as well as the use of both national resources and Union instruments in order to carry them out (Art.I-41.4). When the Council entrusts the implementation of a Petersberg task to a group of member states, 'those Member States, in association with the Union Minister for Foreign Affairs, shall agree among themselves on the management of the task' (Art.III-310).

The European Foreign Minister: an assessment
The advantages and disadvantages arising for the European Union from the envisaged post of European Foreign Minister are inextricably linked. Rightly, the Constitutional Treaty's drafters wanted the Minister to function as a conduit between the actors who contribute to the EU's external policies. He or she would thus help ensure greater coherence and consistency in the external action of the Union. The Constitutional Treaty goes some way to facilitating coherence and consistency, but the price paid is to create a Foreign Minister with a range of institutional masters. In effect, the Minister would be embedded by the Constitutional Treaty somewhere between three European institutions; the European Council, the Council of Ministers and the Commission.

The Minister chairs the Foreign Affairs Council and carries out its instructions. Members of this Council, particularly from the larger member states, are powerful and influential political figures in their right. The Minister would be both subordinate to and a co-equal with the President of the European Council, who according to the Constitutional Treaty is also responsible for ensuring the external representation of the EU in matters concerning CFSP. The European Foreign Minister would be a member of the European Commission reporting on at least some of his activities to the President of the Commission. The Minister must also be obliged to keep the European Parliament informed on a regular basis about the main aspects and basic choices of the Union's external policies.

These potential institutional and personal sensitivities in the Foreign Minister's role have led to the often-repeated observation that the choice of first occupant or occupants of the post would be decisive for the success of the new CFSP system. Only an experienced figure having the confidence of the heads of government and foreign ministers would be able to agree a workable division of representative and other functions with the Presidents of the European Council and the European Commission. The relationship of the Minister with the Commission President might be particularly challenging. The president's role in the Minister's appointment and dismissal is marginal at best. The Minister is entitled to co-ordinate the activities of his or her colleagues in the Commission in their external policies, a power traditionally reserved for the President. The Commission will, if the Constitutional Treaty is ever ratified, be unable to submit any initiative to the Council concerning CFSP without the agreement of the Minister.

Despite these obvious difficulties, few observers doubt that the post of EU Foreign Minister offers a real chance to move towards a better co-ordinated and more effective role for the European Union in the wider world. Combining the roles of the High Representative and the External Affairs Commissioner in one person is an obvious step towards more coherence and convergence in external policy between the Commission and the Council than has been the case in the past. The abolition of the rotating Presidency in the external action field is a real gain for the stability and solidity of European foreign policy. Despite some unclarified divisions of representative responsibility with the President of the European Council and the President of the Commission, there seems little doubt that the European Foreign Minister could be a significant factor for greater visibility and continuity in the external representation of the Union. The high degree of intergovernmentalist procedures which will in any event continue to characterise the Union's CFSP will naturally constrain the autonomous capacity of the Minister. But his enhanced competences envisaged under the Constitutional Treaty would undoubtedly make it easier for the Union to agree on more (and more coherent) decisions of external policy and to represent them more effectively to third parties.

A Foreign Minister without the Constitutional Treaty?

Given that the proposed setting up of the European Union's Foreign Minister reflected a widespread perception among member states that the Union's external action needed to be more coherent and effective, it has been asked whether it might be possible to institute the post of Foreign Minister independently of the European Constitutional Treaty. A number of legal and political barriers, however, stand in the way of any such initiative. The creation of the position of EU Foreign Minister is linked to a whole series of reforms in the external action field. The Treaty on European Union states clearly that it is the rotating Presidency who shall 'represent the Union in matters coming within the common foreign and security policy' (Art.18.1) and 'be responsible for the implementation of decisions taken under this title' (Art.18.2).[8] An amendment of the Treaty would therefore be necessary to exclude the rotating Presidency from the external action field. There is also currently a legal impediment to combining the positions of the High Representative and of the

External Relations Commissioner in one person. Article 213.2 of the Treaty of Rome forbids members of the Commission to 'engage in any other occupation'[9] , a stipulation incompatible with the proposed "double-hatting" of the Foreign Minister.

Given this difficult legal background, consideration is being given to ways of enhancing the authority of the High Representative, possibly by delegating some of the Presidency's tasks to Javier Solana, the already nominated candidate as first Foreign Minister. It has been proposed, for instance, that Mr. Solana should sometimes be invited informally to chair the General Affairs and External Relations Council. This might be particularly appropriate when matters are on the agenda, such as the Western Balkans and the Middle East, where he has a particular expertise. Equally, Mr. Solana could assume on an ad hoc basis more responsibility for external representation. The present triumvirate or troika system comprising the Council Presidency, the High Representative and the External Relations Commissioner, causes confusion in the rest of the world through the changing composition of the troika. Although he cannot entirely replace the troika, the High Representative might be encouraged more often to replace or accompany it as an equal partner. Nor is there any compelling reason why Mr. Solana should not be given an informal right of initiative within the General Affairs Council. If by an Inter-institutional Agreement the rotating Presidency were ready in certain circumstances to put forward as initiatives of the Presidency proposals emanating in reality from the High Representative, then that would reinforce the prestige and influence of Mr. Solana and his successors.

Cumulatively, such incremental steps (combined with administrative measures for better co-ordination between the Commission, Council and member states) might contribute to enhancing the visibility and authority of the High Representative. They would be unlikely however to bring about the enhanced unity and coherence of the EU's external action which the creation of a Foreign Minister for the EU was intended to promote. For legal and political reasons, it seems in the highest degree unlikely that such a post will be instituted without a change to the existing European treaties, whether in the form of a renegotiated Constitutional Treaty or in the form of discrete amendments to the existing European Treaties. Within the Constitutional Treaty, the provisions relating to the CFSP were not the most controversial, either at the level of governments or electorates. Many governments were reassured by the continuing intergovernmental nature of the CFSP under the Treaty and the foreign policy of the European Union played little or no role in negative outcomes of the French and Dutch referendums on the Treaty in 2005. It is certainly difficult to believe that any renegotiated Constitutional Treaty would contain provisions on the European Foreign Minister very different to those agreed by the European Council at Dublin in 2004. The EU's heads of government will need to agree in due course on their next step. They can decide to reincorporate into a new Constitutional Treaty these provisions, adopt them separately as amendments to the existing treaties or abandon the project of a European Foreign Minister altogether. They seem to have no other options.

The External Action Service
In fulfilling his or her mandate, the European Foreign Minister was to be, according to the Constitutional Treaty, assisted by an European External Action Service, which would comprise officials from relevant departments of the Council and of the Commission as well as staff seconded from the diplomatic services of the member states. This new institution had been proposed by the Constitutional Convention, where its first advocates were the former Italian Prime Minister Guiliano Amato and two MEPs, Elmar Brok (Germany) and Andrew Duff (UK).[10] The concept rapidly

gained ground within the Convention and was enshrined in the draft Constitutional Treaty proposed by the Convention to the Intergovernmental Conference. But the Convention's agreement on the general principle of an External Service was despite important differences within its ranks on the nature and working of the Service. In their original initiative, Amato, Brok and Duff had proposed to the Convention that the External Service form part of the European Commission's bureaucratic structure. This was not acceptable to those in the Convention who see the Common Foreign and Security Policy as being primarily an intergovernmental arrangement. This disparity of views within the Convention was left unresolved in the draft Constitutional Treaty, which said that 'the organisation and functioning of the European External Service would be "established by a European decision of the Council' and that the Council would 'act on a proposal from the Union Minister for Foreign Affairs after consulting the European Parliament and after obtaining the consent of the Commission'.[11]

When the EU member states finally adopted the Constitutional Treaty, they did not change the content of the Convention's proposals on the External Service. Significantly, however, the relevant article was placed in the CFSP Chapter in Part III of the Treaty (Art.III-296 para.3). Arguably, this positioning in the Treaty limits the External Service simply to CFSP matters, a limitation which contradicts a central objective of the External Service, namely to integrate and consolidate the EU's whole range of external action instruments. Since the External Service is to assist the Foreign Minister, the Service's scope of action should logically reproduce that of the Foreign Minister.

After the signing of the Constitutional Treaty, the member states decided that preparations should begin immediately for the setting up of the External Service. This instruction was taken up by Javier Solana working together with the Commission, notably José Barroso. At the Brussels European

Council in December 2004, the EU member states urged the Commission and Mr. Solana 'to continue this preparatory work, in particular by identifying key issues, including the scope and structure of the future service'. While doing so, Mr. Barroso and Mr. Solana needed 'to ensure the full involvement of Member States in this process'. They were further instructed to 'prepare a joint progress report' for the June 2005 European Council.[12]

During the first half of 2005, the EU's member states and institutions refined their ideas on the European External Service. Controversy centred on two main questions, the institutional 'location' of the Service and its organisation. The European Parliament demanded in its report of May 2005 that the Service should be 'incorporated, in organisational and budgetary terms, in the Commission's staff structure.'[13] During the debates leading up to the report of May 2005, however, it had become clear that differing opinions existed within the Parliament on this issue. Lamberto Dini (Italy) and Klaus Haensch (Germany), for instance, argued that the most natural interpretation of the Constitutional Treaty was that the Service should be a sui generis entity, based on none of the existing European institutional models. Among the EU member states, there was no enthusiasm for the Service to become part of the Commission, and no obvious support for locating it in the Secretariat General of the Council. The European Commission also recognised that its preferred solution, the incorporation of the External Service into the Commission itself, was unattainable.

Intertwined with the controversy about the institutional affiliation of the Service were the questions of its composition and organisation. If the Service were to be incorporated into the Commission or the Secretariat of the Council, significant reorganisation of these two latter bodies would need to take place. On the other hand, if the External Service were to be established autonomously of the Commission or the Council, some duplication of work by staff already engaged in the Commission and Council would be the inevitable consequence. The background was further complicated by the disparity in present staffing levels between the institutions. The Commission has over 3000 staff members working in the three Directorates-General most directly engaged in external action, while the Council has only 225 equivalent staff, supplemented by a further 140 working on the Military Staff. As provided for in the Helsinki Report, the Military Staff is to provide military expertise and support to the European Security and Defence Policy, including the conduct of EU-led military crisis management operations.

A range of options was considered by Mr. Solana and Mr. Barroso. The organisationally least ambitious approach would have incorporated into the External Action Service only Directorates dealing with the EU's external actions in the Council Secretariat and the Directorate-General for External Relations from the Commission. At the other end of the spectrum, proposals were discussed for bringing together in the External Service all officials dealing with the external action of the Union from the Council and the Commission, and adding to their number the officials who represent the Union in third countries. This body would certainly not lack for resources, but it might be wondered whether the European Foreign Minister would be able adequately to supervise all its activities. A further complication arose from the stipulation of the Constitutional Treaty that the External Service was to compromise not only 'officials from the relevant departments of the General Secretariat of the Council and of the Commission' but also 'staff seconded from national diplomatic service of the member states'. How many such staff should be detached to the Service, and whether their terms of employment should be the same as those for Council and Commission officials were obviously controversial problems. According to the Constitutional Treaty, the external delegations of the European Union were to be placed under the authority of the European Foreign

Minister, without its being made clear whether their staff belonged to the External Service. Until now, these external delegations have been confined by the member states to the task of representing exclusively the European Commission in (usually) national capitals.

The first draft of the joint progress report to be written by Solana and Barroso was presented in March 2005 as a basis for discussions with EU member states. This draft acknowledged that the signatories of the Constitutional Treaty may have foreseen a sui generis status for the External Service, and asked the EU member states to make proposals as to what this status should be. In the view of Solana and Barroso, the External Service should incorporate those services presently working in CFSP areas within the Council and the Commission as well as the military staff from the Council. The Service needed to comprise 'geographical desks which cover all the countries/regions of the world' and 'single thematic desks [...], on issues such as human rights, counter-terrorism, non-proliferation and relations with international organisations such as the UN' in order to support not only the European Foreign Minister, but also the other Commissioners and the President of the European Council. Areas such as trade, enlargement and development policy would, however, be excluded from the External Service's remit. The draft paper made no recommendations on the external delegations of the EU, or on the budget to fund the External Service.[14]

Between March and June 2005, Solana and Barroso made some progress on finding consensual solutions among the member states on outstanding issues relating to the Service. The great majority of member states envisaged a sui generis status for the Service, 'under the authority of the Foreign Minister, with close links to both the Council and the Commission'. Most of the member states agreed with the organisation of the Service proposed by Solana and Barroso, namely to include in it the services dealing with CFSP in the

Commission and in the Council, and to set up within its internal structure both geographical and thematic desks. The member states also agreed that external delegations should be an integral part of the External Service, although most member states thought this did not imply that 'all staff working in the delegations would need to be members of the [External Service]'. A majority (but not all) of the member states supported the idea that at some time in the future the Union Delegations might perform additional tasks such as consular protection and visas. Concerning the staff seconded from the member states to the External Service, most member states argued that their national diplomats should become 'temporary agents' of the Service in order to guarantee that 'all staff in the External Service had the same status and conditions of employment.' The financing of the External Service remained unresolved. Their report laconically concludes that budgetary issues required further examination.[15]

The External Action Service: an assessment
It is obvious from the discussions about the European External Service in 2004 and 2005 that the member states have differing expectations among themselves as to the likely advantages of the External Service. Some see it as an essentially co-ordinating body between other powerful actors on the European stage, others see it as an embryonic European Foreign Ministry and others see it simply as a potential way of saving money and other resources. Smaller member states, indeed, hope that in the medium term it may be possible for the External Service to take over some at least of the representative and analytical functions currently fulfilled by their own expensive and over-stretched diplomatic services.

Larger member states such as the United Kingdom and France tend to be less sanguine, inclined sometimes to view the External Service as a potential rival to their national diplomacies. Ironically, this suspicion co-exists, at least in the United Kingdom, with a more positive view of the External Service, as working to the Council primarily and therefore as a possible counterbalance to the increasing external profile of the European Commission. The former British Foreign Secretary, Jack Straw, remarked that 'you find all sorts of odd bods from the European Union running all sorts of odd offices around the world and that it would be a good thing if arrangements for the European External Service gave us more control than we have at the moment'.[16]

The External Service has also been a source of contention between the European Parliament, the Commission and the Council Secretariat. These disagreements have principally concerned the institutional design and specific duties of the External Service and not the underlying desirability of the new body. It is common ground between the European institutions (as distinct from some of the member states) that the External Service will fulfil a worthwhile and necessary role in providing a platform for facilitating dialogue and co-ordination among the external actors of the European Union and contributing towards the ultimate goal of consensus-building.

The External Service is a serious attempt to improve co-ordination, the equivalent at the official and administrative level of the European Foreign Minister. If a coherent European external action demands a single figure to articulate it, then that single figure must logically need for the formulation and refinement of European external action a single organisation primarily responsible to him or her. In the year 2000 Javier Solana drew an interesting comparison between the 14123 American diplomats scattered throughout the world in 300 missions and the 39000 European diplomats in 1500 missions, and ironically wondered whether Europe was a more powerful diplomatic force than the USA in consequence.[17] Solana clearly does not think it is and is no doubt implying that some at least of the European diplomats perform unnecessary or fruitlessly competitive tasks. The

23

arguments in favour of at least some progress towards an External Action Service are practical as well as political.

An External Action Service without the Constitutional Treaty?

After the rejection of the Constitutional Treaty by the French and Dutch voters, the European Council of June 2005 decided not to consider the Solana/Barroso report on the External Service. A number of member states had feared that the continuation of work to set up the Service might be interpreted by voters as a rejection of the negative outcome of the consultations in France and the Netherlands. Other member states, by contrast, have expressed the hope that it might be possible to introduce the European External Service without the Constitutional Treaty. They have argued that no substantial legal or administrative obstacles remain in the way of setting up the External Service. If the European institutions wished to do so they could conclude among themselves inter-institutional agreements to facilitate, as the Nice Treaty puts it, 'the application of the provisions of the Treaty establishing the European Community'.[18] Admittedly, such agreements may not "amend or supplement" the provisions of the existing European Treaties. But advocates of the immediate setting-up of the proposed External Service believe that it should be possible to bring the Service into being without running the risk of legal challenge on this ground.

Even if it is true that the Service could be set up by an Inter-institutional Agreement, the current impasse over the ratification of the Constitutional Treaty nevertheless acts as a considerable barrier to the mobilisation of the necessary political will to conclude such an agreement. Replying to a question from the British Member of the European Parliament, Charles Tannock, the British Presidency of the Union said in September 2005 that the establishment of the European External Service is one of the provisions of the Constitutional Treaty; as such, it shall take effect only when the Treaty itself comes into force. This negative reaction certainly reflects the desire of the British government to talk and think as little as possible about the Constitutional Treaty after being saved from a difficult referendum on the Treaty in Britain by the French and Dutch votes. Until now, there has been little political momentum visible behind the often voiced view of academic and other commentators that the creation of a European External Service is an attractive and relatively easily achieved element of the Constitutional Treaty for 'cherry-picking'. The public view of most member states is still that an attempt should still be made to ratify something like the existing European Constitutional Treaty. However, if the European Council ever concludes that the Constitution should not or cannot be ratified in its present form, and the member states decide to make a concerted effort to rescue on an ad hoc basis what can be rescued from the wreckage of the Constitutional Treaty, the European External Service would clearly be an attractive candidate for such a rescue.

A European Foreign Policy?

Brendan Donnelly, Stephen Haseler & Jeannette Ladzik

European Security and Defence Policy

Established at the Cologne European Council in June 1999, the European Security and Defence Policy (ESDP) has, in the 7 years since its inception, given rise to countless debates and discussions. Whereas some commentators regard the ESDP as an overall success story, others voice doubts. The discussion about whether the EU should send peacekeeping troops to the Democratic Republic of Congo during elections this June seemed for many to crystallise these doubts. Only three EU member states would have been capable of leading such a mission, and two of them, France and the United Kingdom, were unwilling and unable to mount an international deployment because of their respective involvement in Iraq and the Ivory Coast. For long, it was a matter of high public controversy in Germany whether the country should undertake the proposed mission to Africa. It was only with a narrow majority in the Bundestag that eventually the decision was taken.

Such uncertainty is not calculated to increase Europe's standing and military credibility in the world. On the other hand, the European Security and Defence Policy has undoubted successes to its credit. The creation of a Rapid Reaction Force, the gradual evolution of the EU Battlegroups and the European Police Force and the EU's first major security mission to Bosnia-Herzegovina have exceeded the expectations of the cynics. Political, financial and material problems continue to plague the ESDP, but there has undoubtedly been progress over the past seven years.

Background

A European Security and Defence Policy has been a European ambition for some decades. However, the legal basis for such a policy was only laid down with the adoption of the Maastricht Treaty in 1991, which instituted the Common Foreign and Security Policy 'including the eventual framework of a common defence policy, which might in time lead to a common defence'.[19] In 1997, the Amsterdam Treaty changed this provision to envisage the 'progressive' framing of a common European defence policy.

The Maastricht and Amsterdam Treaties provided however only the treaty framework for an emerging European Security and Defence Policy. The ultimate launch pad for its establishment was the EU's dismal performance during the Balkan crises of the 1990s and the Bosnia and Kosovo conflicts in particular, when it was the United States and NATO who contributed decisively to the pacification of a region 'on the European Union's doorstep'. This humiliating experience generated increasing frustration from the EU's member states over Europe's military impotence and dependence on the US. In particular, it served as a catalyst for bringing the UK and France closer together on defence questions.

In December 1998, at a Franco-British summit in Saint Malo, the two member states released a Joint Declaration, in which for the first time it was stressed that the EU must have 'the capacity for autonomous action, backed up by credible military forces'. Following this meeting, the Cologne European Council of June 1999 agreed to implement this Joint Declaration and give reality to the concept of a European Security and Defence Policy.

Helsinki Headline Goal

Prior to the European Council summit in Helsinki in December 1999, French President Jacques Chirac and British Prime Minister Tony Blair held another meeting, at which they urged the EU to strive for the capacity to deploy rapidly and then sustain combat forces which could be militarily self-sufficient up to corps level, an ambitious target involving thousands, rather than simply handfuls of troops. These Anglo-French recommendations were accepted by the member states at the Helsinki European Council of 1999, at which it was agreed to launch the Helsinki Headline Goal, calling for the creation of a functioning Rapid Reaction Force (RRF) of up to 60,000 troops with naval and air support by 2003. The Rapid Reaction Force should be deployable at full strength within 60 days of a deployment decision and be sustainable in the field for at least one year. Furthermore, the RRF must be able to act upon the full range of the so-called 'Petersberg tasks', which embrace humanitarian missions, peacekeeping, and combat tasks in crisis management, including the making (not merely the maintenance) of peace.

In order to meet the Helsinki Headline Goal two catalogues were drawn up in the wake of the Helsinki Council: the first listed the capabilities required to achieve the Headline Goal, the second the units voluntarily earmarked by the member states at a Capability Commitment Conference held in Brussels in November 2000. When both lists had been completed, it was clear that an enormous gap existed between the required and the actual offered capabilities. Accordingly, at a further conference held in Brussels in November 2001 the EU member states adopted a European Capability Action Plan (ECAP) 'incorporating all the efforts, investments, developments and co-ordination measures executed or planned at both national and multinational level with a view to improving existing resources and gradually developing the capabilities necessary for the Union's envisaged activities in ESDP.'[20]

When the first phase of the Capability Action Plan was concluded in May 2003, further disappointment awaited the member states. It became clear at that date that little real progress had been made on moving the Rapid Reaction Force closer to reality. This was mainly because the European Capability Action Plan had allowed considerable flexibility to the member states, permitting them to decide on an ad hoc basis when and how additional capabilities should be allocated. Despite these shortcomings, the EU defence ministers declared in May 2003 that the EU now had initial operational capability across the full range of Petersberg tasks, although they acknowledged that the capabilities were limited and constrained, particularly in the key areas of rapid deployment, sustainability and concurrent operations. For their part, the member states recognised failings in the implementation of the Action Plan and agreed on improvements including regular reviews during each Presidency of progress made (or not) towards capability improvement. Critics noted that national governments still retained for themselves a large measure of discretion in the future implementation of the Plan. These critics also pointed out that most of the armed forces allocated to the EU can only be deployed to observer and peacekeeping missions of low intensity, with specialised combat troops being in noticeably short supply. Moreover, strategic lift assets are still lacking, causing difficulties of deployment and sustainability, especially for distant missions.

Headline Goal 2010

Against this background, the Council proposed in its ESDP Presidency Report 2003 that 'in addition to the outstanding capability shortfalls against the Helsinki Headline Goal', the EU should now 'set new goals for the further development of European capabilities for crisis management with a horizon of 2010'.[21] The new goals should take into account the current limitations and constraints and, more importantly, the new European Security Strategy. The European Security Strategy, which was adopted by the European Council in December 2003, was designed to show that the EU could become a strategic actor, to promote a common understanding within the EU regarding security risks the EU is facing today, and to provide the means to confront these challenges. At the European Council summit in June 2004, the EU member states agreed to adopt the new Headline Goal 2010, which should focus on the qualitative aspects of capability development, in particular interoperability, deployability and sustainability. These three factors should be at the core of member states' efforts to improve military capabilities.

Since only part of the European armed forces can currently be deployed at high readiness as a response to a crisis, the Headline Goal 2010 envisages in particular further development of the EU's capacity for rapid decision-making in the planning and deployment of forces. 'The ambition of the EU under the Headline Goal is to be able to take the decision to launch an operation within 5 days of the approval of the Crisis Management Concept by the Council. The relevant forces should be able to start implementing their mission on the ground no later than 10 days after the EU decision to launch the operation.'[22]

Central to the EU's aspirations under the 2010 Headline Goal is the Battlegroup concept, a British-French-German proposal. In February 2004, the three states jointly submitted a 'Food for Thought Paper', which suggested producing a 'catalogue of high utility force packages that can be tailored rapidly to specific missions'.[23] These 'packages' rapidly came to be known as 'Battlegroups' and the concept was officially launched at the 2004 Capability Commitment Conference. Each Battlegroup is based on a combined arms, battalion-size force (1,500 troops) reinforced with combat support and combat service support. Since the Battlegroups should be sustainable in the field for 30 days, extendable to even 120 days, they will be capable of stand-alone operations or for the initial phase of large operations. Battlegroups will be employable across the full range of both the Petersberg tasks as listed in the Treaty on the European Union (TEU) Art.17.2 and those identified in the European Security Strategy. They are designed specifically, but not exclusively, to be used in response to a request from the UN. Battlegroups can be either national or multinational, i.e. composed of troops from one or more member states. Interoperability will be the hoped-for key to their military effectiveness.

At the Capability Commitment Conference of 2004, member states made an initial commitment to the formation of 13 Battlegroups. Four member states (UK, France, Italy and Spain) provided their national Battlegroups at an early stage of the programme, and in 2006 a German-French Battlegroup with contributions from Belgium, Luxembourg and Spain had achieved partial operational capability for evacuation and extraction. From January 2007, the EU will have the full operational capability to undertake two Battlegroup-size rapid response operations, including the ability to launch both operations almost simultaneously. Only Denmark and Malta are currently not participating in any Battlegroup. In February 2006, Ireland's Minister of Defence Willie O'Dea signalled Ireland's future participation in the Battlegroups.

Many in and outside Europe hope that the Battlegroups will spur the EU member states to increase capabilities, since the Battlegroups are not based simply on re-arranging existing capabilities, but also on producing new ones. Questions, however, remain as to the long-term viability of the concept. Transport and political decision-making when troops are confronted with a rapidly changing situation on the ground are areas of likely especial difficulty. The substantial political will shown until now for the realisation of the Battlegroup concept gives ground for hope that these problems may gradually be capable of solution.

Problems

The rapid reaction force and the Battlegroups are definite, if limited steps towards a more credible role for the EU in global crisis management. There are, however, still a range of shortcomings to address before the EU can meet its objectives as set out in the European Security Strategy. The most obvious obstacle derives from the relatively low overall level of military expenditure by the EU's member states. Limited resources have repeatedly constrained the implementation of otherwise promising initiatives decided by the member states. In 2004, the US alone spent more than twice as much on defence as all the EU member states combined. Defence spending also varies unevenly among the member states. About 80 per cent of total EU spending and 98 per cent of military R&D expenditure are covered by the six most important arms-producing countries, the UK, France, Germany, Italy, Spain and Sweden.[24]

Moreover, some European defence spending is not invested to the best possible effect. Although a degree of military restructuring has taken place among the member states since the end of the Cold War, they still spend too much on personnel and too little on the acquisition of new equipment and on R&D. Accordingly, most of the forces of EU member states are still in-place forces. When it comes to waging war away from their home base, the European capacity for autonomous action is very limited. In such cases, they must rely on external actors. The recently created European Defence Agency may help the member states eliminate waste in their defence budgets and enhance the effectiveness of existing budgets: the Agency's job is to identify gaps in capability and make recommendations on how those gaps could be filled. The Agency is of course a newcomer among the European Union's institutions. It remains to be seen how far it can achieve its mission and significantly support the member states in their effort to improve European defence capabilities in the field of crisis management.

Powerful objective arguments can be advanced in support of the proposition that the best way for EU member states to increase their military capabilities would be through the greatest possible degree of defence integration. Budget pressures and increasing ambitions in the defence field are natural pointers towards national specialisation and pooling of limited resources. According to the European Security Strategy, 'systematic use of pooled and shared assets would reduce duplications, overheads, and, in the medium-term, increase capabilities'.[25] Pooling has proven especially attractive to some member states since it allows them to preserve national autonomy whilst generating cost-effective solutions. Specialisation in 'niche' capabilities is attractive in particular for smaller European countries.

As always, the EU's member states will need over the coming decade to decide what is the balance they wish to strike in the defence field between national independence and the enhanced collective capacity generated by further integration. The balance sought will not necessarily be the same for the governments of all member states, although polls suggest that public opinion throughout the European Union is strikingly willing to accept further integration in the sphere of security and defence policies.

Civilian Capabilities

The creation of the European Security and Defence Policy has put pressure on the classic notion of the EU as an exclusively civilian power. But in parallel to its military capabilities, the EU's civilian capabilities have also evolved in recent years, capabilities that have a definite contribution to make to the global actions of the European Union. For instance, at the Feira European Council summit in June 2000, the EU member states listed four priority areas in which the EU should acquire civilian capabilities: police, the rule of law, civil administration and civil protection. The Council's goal was that by 2003 a police force of up to 5,000 personnel contributing to international missions across the range of conflict prevention and crisis management operations should be set up.7 Rapid progress towards this goal was made after the Feira summit and in consequence the EU was able to take over from the UN's International Police Task Force in Bosnia-Herzegovina in January 2003.

At the European Council summit in December 2004, a Civilian Headline Goal 2008 was endorsed by the EU member states. This Headline Goal envisages the deployment of civilian ESDP capabilities within 30 days of the decision to launch a mission. Examples of activities the civilian operations should carry out include security sector reform and support to disarmament and demobilisation processes.[26] In the ESDP Presidency Report 2005[27] , consensus was reached on a concept for setting up and deploying civilian response teams with the initial goal of a pool of up to 100 experts by the end of 2006. The objectives of such teams are early assessments of a crisis situation, support for the establishment of civilian ESDP missions and support to an EU special representative or an ongoing civilian operation. The teams should be mobilised and deployed within 5 days of a request.

Besides the development of separate military and civilian capabilities, the EU has recently attempted to co-ordinate both these capabilities better. In the ESDP Presidency Report 2005, UK, Austria and Finland set out an approach by which civil-military co-ordination would be taken forward during their Presidencies. In parallel, the Political and Security Committee introduced a Concept for Comprehensive Planning, which addresses the need for effective co-ordination of activity by all relevant EU actors in crisis management. Post-Cold War conflict response certainly requires an effective marrying up of both civilian and military aspects in the operational phase. The Union is aware of this need, even if opportunities to run such integrated missions have not yet presented themselves.

With 4 completed and 10 ongoing operations, the EU has

proved that it is able to carry out military or civilian operations in a number of different regions of the world. The first-ever mission launched was the ESDP police mission in Bosnia-Herzegovina, mentioned above. The first military mission, which took place in the Former Yugoslav Republic of Macedonia, put the 'Berlin-plus' agreement between NATO and the EU into practice, with the EU drawing on NATO assets and capabilities during this operation. The so-called Concordia Mission lasted from March to December 2003. During that time, the EU was able to create a stable and secure environment in Macedonia.

A real turning point for the EU was Operation Artemis in the Democratic Republic of Congo, which lasted from July to September 2003. Not only was it the first autonomous military mission and the first operation in Africa, but the EU also managed to act quickly and effectively. Within a week after the UN Secretary General Kofi Annan asked the EU to help, the Council had approved the mission, with troops on the ground a few days later. Although Operation Artemis involved only 1800 (mostly French) soldiers and lasted a mere 2 months before the EU handed full responsibility back to the UN, the operation was in all respects a success. The mission restored the security situation and disarmed local militias, allowing a large number of refugees to return. Most importantly, the EU showed through Operation Artemis that its decision-making and military planning organs were able to execute rapidly a purely EU operation in a case of an emergency situation in a demanding theatre of operation.

Out of the three military missions the EU has conducted so far, Operation Althea in Bosnia-Herzegovina is the largest one. A robust force of 7,000 troops was deployed in December 2004 to Bosnia-Herzegovina to take over from NATO's SFOR. Although the operation is being carried out with recourse to NATO assets and capabilities on the basis of the 'Berlin plus' agreement, Althea can be regarded as a new step in the development of ESDP in terms of size and ambition. The objectives of the still ongoing operation are to provide deterrence, to uphold security and stability, and to ensure compliance with the Dayton Peace Accord. The military mission is also linked to the police mission already in place in Bosnia-Herzegovina. This attempt to co-ordinate the civilian and military approach potentially marks the beginning of an encouraging new phase in the EU's crisis management. Optimists about the future development of the ESDP point out that in Bosnia-Herzegovina the European Union has replaced the former dominant power, the United States. The European Union may wish and need in coming years to act as a guarantor for stability in a number of areas where the United States has until now performed this role.

Conclusion

Because the European Security and Defence Policy is primarily intergovernmental in character, its development depends crucially upon the continuing political will of the EU member states, notably the bigger member states. Despite real successes, there are still political, doctrinal and financial problems which may hinder unless resolved the ESDP from meeting its own ambitions set out in the European Security Strategy. For example, the accession of the former Eastern Bloc countries has cast new light on the debate about crisis management. The new member states tend to regard NATO as the most important military alliance in which they participate and can sometimes see ESDP as a distraction from, or even a threat to, the all-important Atlantic link. Some such thinking can also on occasion be discerned in the ranks of 'old Europe'.

Moreover, the European Union still lacks an overall strategic concept for crisis management. Its operations have been episodic and occasional, with no clearly defined statement of long-term objectives or geostrategic analysis. The adoption of the European Security Strategy was a step in the right direction, but its focus was contemporary rather than oriented towards the shaping of a future world in a way most reflective of European interests and aspirations. The suspension of the Union's ratification process for the Constitutional Treaty is an undoubted setback towards this goal. The Treaty included in its provisions the inchoate concept of 'structured co-operation' in the military field between member states that had already achieved a high level of military preparedness. A number of questions were left unanswered by the Treaty about the scope and implementation of this new concept. But its adoption through the Treaty would and have been a forceful spur to further reflection and analysis.

Finally, and inevitably, questions of finance remain for the ESDP's operation. To date, the EU has strictly separated purely or mainly civilian operations, which are charged to the budget of the Community, and 'operations having military or defence implications', which are charged to the member states in accordance with a GNP-scale, unless the Council unanimously decides otherwise (Art.28 TEU).[28] Since today peace building tasks require a mix of military and civilian components such a separation is artificial and unsustainable. In reality, individual missions of the EU under ESDP have been financed on an ad hoc and unpredictable basis. Political will has been able to overcome real but essentially secondary problems of accounting and contributions.

Common Commercial Policy

Historical background

The passive role of the Commission in CFSP and ESDP stands in contrast to the major part the Commission plays in the Common Commercial Policy. This policy field has been a stronghold of the Commission since the early days of integration, although a continuous reluctance on the part of the member states to grant the Commission the necessary autonomy to negotiate on behalf of the Council has also been a recurrent feature.

The 1957 Treaty of Rome provided for the development of a Common External Tariff (CET) and a Common Commercial Policy, establishing uniform principles between the member states governing EU trade policy including changes in tariff rates, export policy and instruments to protect trade such as anti-dumping measures. The definition, scope and objectives of the Common Commercial Policy were set out in the articles 110-116 of the founding treaty. Under these Articles, the Commission holds the exclusive right to propose policies and where agreements with third countries require to be negotiated, the Commission is authorised by the Council to conduct the necessary negotiations (Art.113). The Commission, however, only acts as the sole negotiator in matters falling under Art.113, 'exclusive Community competence'. In regards to issues falling under mixed competence, ad hoc solutions have had to be found. During the entire process of negotiations, the Commission is assisted by a committee (Art.113 Committee) appointed by the Council, which can modify the mandate on minor technical points. The results on international trade agreements are adopted by the Council. In those areas covered by Article 113, the Council approves the agreements by qualified majority vote. In case of mixed competence, unanimity applies. Furthermore, where competence is shared, the Council members sign the relevant trade agreements in addition to the Commission and national ratification procedures apply.

The most important testing-ground for the application of the Common Commercial Policy over the past thirty years was the Uruguay Round, the trade negotiation which lasted from 1986 to 1994 and transformed the 'General Agreement on Tariffs and Trade' (GATT) into the 'World Trade Organisation' (WTO). The Commission believed that for these negotiations it had been assigned the role of the sole negotiator on behalf of the Community and its member states. Yet from the outset it was unclear whether the 'Trade-Related Aspects of Intellectual Property' (TRIPS) and a 'General Agreement on Trade in Services' (GATS), which were for the first time included in the negotiations, were part of the competence of the Community or of its member states. When it came to the signing of the results of the Uruguay Round in 1994, the member states insisted on signing the final document in addition to the Commission.

As a result of this conflict of competences, the Commission submitted after the Uruguay Round a request to the European Court of Justice to review the question of competence and scope of Article 113. The Commission attempted to achieve judicially what it had failed to achieve politically: a recognition of the Community's exclusive competence in the area of external policy covered by the WTO. As it turned out, Opinion 1/94 of the European Court of Justice was a severe setback for the Commission. The Court ruled that the Community and the member states are jointly competent to conclude GATS or TRIPS agreements.

The Amsterdam Treaty was a further disappointment for the Commission, since the member states only agreed on introducing a small reform of the Commercial Policy's scope. The Treaty created a new procedure, whereby services and intellectual property could become part of the European Union's exclusive competences. The threshold for attaining exclusive competence in services and intellectual property, however, was placed very high: unanimity was needed to transfer competence from the member states to the Community. This procedure did not apply to the related, but contentious issue of foreign direct investment.

The Amsterdam 'fast track' possibility was replaced by a new paragraph in the Nice Treaty allowing for trade in services and commercial aspects of intellectual property to be negotiated and concluded under exclusive competence of the Community if the member states, by qualified majority, decide so. The member states however listed a series of conditions in order to restrict the potential increase in the scope of application. Agreements relating to trade in cultural and audiovisual services, educational services, and social and human health services, still fall within the shared competence of the Community and its Member States.

Over time, a sui generis decision-making system in the Common Commercial Policy has developed, characterised by the emergence of formal and informal rules biased to some degree to the 'Community method'. However, since the 1990s attempts by the member states to 're-nationalise' trade policy have intensified. In the recent Doha round, successive European Commissioners Pascal Lamy and Peter Mandelson were influential and authoritative figures in global international trade negotiations. Throughout the negotiations, however, individual member states regularly expressed their unease at the manner and content of the Commission's actions on their behalf.

The Constitutional Treaty and Community competence in CCP

The Common Commercial Policy was a topic considered by the European Constitutional Convention, although it was clearly regarded as being less important than the Common Foreign and Security Policy. Art.III-217 para1 of the Convention's draft Treaty stipulated that the 'Common Commercial Policy shall be conducted in the context of the principles and objectives of the Union's external action'.[29] Decision-making in trade policy was also to be changed, with the scope of the CCP redefined, greater use of qualified majority voting being proposed and the European Parliament more fully involved. The exceptions recognised in the Nice Treaty were either abolished or reduced and the implementation of the CCP subject the Union's normal legislative procedure. In short, the Convention envisaged something very like the wholesale "communitarisation" of the Common Commercial Policy.

Surprisingly to some observers, the Intergovernmental Conference largely endorsed the proposals of the European Constitutional Convention relating to the Common Commercial Policy. The Constitutional Treaty stipulates that the Commission does not have the exclusive competence to negotiate, conclude or implement an international agreement on areas of policy where the Union does not have the power to legislate internally; and some proposals of the Convention for extending qualified majority within the CCP were rejected. But the overall effect of the Constitutional Treaty would have been to make of the CCP an almost perfect example of the "Community method" applied to external decision-making.

The Constitutional Treaty would have strengthened the position of the European Community's institutions in the Common Commercial Policy by an extension of application of the qualified majority voting procedure in the Council, involvement of the European Parliament, and by transferring some fields of shared competences into those within the Union's exclusive competence.[30] GATS and TRIPS for example would under the Treaty no longer fall partly within the competence of the European Community or within the competence of the member states, but would fall within the competence of the Union. This would assure the unitary representation of interests within the WTO for the first time. The proposed changes tended towards greater centralisation of trade policy and towards reducing the influence of the member states.

Two main factors were at work during the Convention and the Intergovernmental Conference to favour changes in the CCP which would have been much less likely five years previously. The continuing Doha Round of the WTO, which was the background to both Convention and Conference, was a standing reminder to member states of the need for efficient and speedy decision-making if the EU was to make a major contribution to these negotiations. In general, the WTO is a forum where the advantages which accrue to the Union from speaking with one voice, that of the European Commission, are particularly easy to discern. This analysis has only been reinforced in the minds of many member states by the enlargement of the Union in 2004. During the Convention and IGC enlargement was often cited as a rationale for greater centralisation of decision-making in the CCP, for fear that twenty five or twenty seven national vetoes would simply be a recipe for paralysis. The twin pressures from an evolving world trade agenda and from the enlargement of the Union were reinforced in the Convention's discussions at least by the influential role in that forum which representatives of the Union's supranational institutions were able to play.

Future international trade agreements, even under the Constitutional Treaty, would still have required unanimous agreement from the member states of the Union. But the negotiation and implementation of these agreements would have been much more unified and centralised than before.

Increase of the Community's competences in CCP without the Constitutional Treaty?

In the debate on the Constitutional Treaty in several member states it became clear that opposition to the Treaty was often founded upon a rejection of the economic philosophy which, rightly or wrongly, the Treaty was held to incorporate. In France in particular, it was argued that acceptance of the Treaty would hasten the dismantling of the European social model, and encourage a move towards neo-liberal policies throughout Europe. Although this analysis centred particularly on the Treaty's sections relating to employment and social policy, the increasing competence of the Union in the Common Commercial Policy envisaged by the Treaty was also a concern to many French voters. Fears were often expressed during the referendum campaign in France that the British Trade Commissioner, aided by other apostles of the free market such as Mr. Barroso, were using the WTO negotiations as a weapon to destroy the Common Agricultural Policy, central to French understanding of the European Union and of the French role within the Union.

It is indeed true that over the past decade a number of significant reforms have been introduced into the Common Agricultural Policy and that pressure from the Union's trading partners has been at least one factor in precipitating these changes. National administrations, including that of France, have been prepared at least to acquiesce in this process. Some have even regarded the WTO negotiations as a convenient justification for domestically painful but economically necessary changes to the Common Agricultural Policy. The "Doha" round of trade negotiations was presented as primarily a round designed to help developing countries. The European Union and most of its member states would not have wished to be portrayed as an obstacle to the success of such an enterprise and were prepared to make the concessions necessary (including changes to the Common Agricultural Policy) for the conclusion of the negotiations.

The indefinite suspension of the Doha Round earlier this year, however, and the failure of the Constitutional Treaty in the Dutch and French referendums (partly due in the latter case to the Treaty's provisions on CCP) create a new and less propitious background for any initiatives to move towards greater communitarisation of CCP. Arguably, the Doha Round's failure is part of a larger trend towards economic nationalism in the advanced economies. For domestic political reasons, Washington and Brussels are currently unwilling to open up politically sensitive markets to international competition. Long the major supporter of trade liberalisation in world forums, the US has recently had to adjust to growing economic nationalism in the US, in a way that is likely to result in a slowing of the thrust towards liberalised global markets.

The European Union is also going through a period of increasing economic nationalism. In August 2005, France announced that it would protect from buyouts by foreign companies domestic industries it considers as strategic. The Spanish government has similarly protected its major energy provider, Endesa, from foreign suitors. The takeover of Polish banks by purchasers from other EU countries has also proved domestically controversial. Failing an unexpectedly rapid resumption of the WTO's trade talks, the Constitutional Treaty's proposals in the area of the Common Commercial Policy are likely to remain a dead letter. Even if the Doha Round were revived, it would be far from easy to maintain the Constitutional Treaty's provisions on the Common Commercial Policy in any revised version of the document. French public opinion in particular has now been alerted to

45

the implications of the Treaty's proposed changes in the area of CCP. A French government would think long and hard in future before it signed or submitted to a referendum a Treaty text containing any similar changes. The Common Commercial Policy is an area where there is already a high degree of "communitarisation" in its operation. What has been achieved will not be lost, but further progress in the near future seems unlikely.

Brendan Donnelly, Stephen Haseler & Jeannette Ladzik

The Geostrategic Background

The European-wide debate amongst political leaders, and publics, about European foreign and security policy still tends to revolve around 'domestic' European concerns: traditional arguments about national sovereignty versus supranationalism, or about the balance needed to be struck between welfare and defence. It is a debate that seems to take place in a vacuum as though the big question of CFSP has little to do with the wider world of geo-politics. In fact, no matter the internal obstacles to creating a serious CFSP, it is the rapidly changing geo-political scene that may well hold the key: that can create that elusive European political will needed to drive the project forward.

At the heart of the changing global scene – indeed perhaps its central characteristic – is the weakening of the idea of a 'uni-polar world' guided and dominated by a 'lone super-power' whose writ can run virtually unchallenged. It was this uni-polar analysis (and the associated ideas of hegemony) that fuelled the George W. Bush strategy of American unilateralism and the forward deployment of military power that ended up with the 2003 invasion of Iraq.

At the time, sceptics, both in Europe and also in the US, pointed to the central problem of this analysis: that no nation, no matter its military might, with only 5% of the world's people and 20% of the world's economy can ultimately impose unilaterally-driven solutions. And that, should it try to, it would soon come up against the limits of its power.

The chaotic situation in the Middle East now stands testimony to such limits of power. The US-led invasion of Iraq, with its promise of re-structuring the Middle East through 'democratisation', has instead turned into, at best, a serious set-back for Washington and, at worst, a geo-strategic defeat. As a result of this American debacle, traditional US (and Western) allies in the region, such as Saudi Arabia, Jordan and the Gulf states, have been weakened and Shiite Iran has been strengthened. Also, the recent Israeli-Hezbollah conflict has further weakened America's Middle East position as the military invincibility of the US's main ally, Israel, has, for the first time since the early 1960's, been seriously questioned.

Also, this Middle East imbroglio comes at the same time as a number of signs of US economic weakness. The all-time high double deficits of trade and the federal budget, together with the growing debate about wage stasis and 'outsourcing'- the so-called 'Middle Class squeeze'- are giving the erstwhile robust US economy a certain lack of lustre. Indeed, the US economy is now, partly because of changes in the dollar-euro rate, smaller than the EU economy. And, on present growth rates, China will also be in a position to challenge US economic supremacy- in Asia it already does so – as well as holding the leverage deriving from its vital role as investor in the US economy and Treasury.

In this environment, talk of a 'lone super-power' or of a 'uni-polar moment' is no longer credible. A more realistic global analysis is of the emergence of 'multi-polar world' containing multiple power bases. It is a world in which new economic superpowers – China, India, the EU, possibly Russia (based upon energy) – vie for influence with the USA in a world in which the USA's serious military superiority may no longer be a decisive factor. It is also a world which allows new regional agglomerations of power -such as Asean, Mercosur and the African Union – to play a serious role.

In this new multi-polar world Europe is now a global player and a potential super-power. The EU is already the world's largest single market and boasts a single currency that is rapidly becoming the equal of the dollar (and an alternative reserve currency). Militarily the EU remains weak, but its leading member states are serious military actors, and two of them, Britain and France, are nuclear powers. In international bodies, the UN, the WTO and other world bodies, Europe's voice can be decisive. It is already a great civilian power and in the coming multi-polar age can aspire to becoming a global superpower with all the potential for influencing world events that such power entails. And it will do so in a way that its separate member states can never aspire to. Whilst Europe remains an 'economic giant and political dwarf' Britain will try to influence events through remaining a junior partner of the United States; and France will never be strong enough to become truly independent.

This emerging multi-polar world will in no way herald the collapse of American power, let alone its primacy. Nor will it induce the much-discussed 'isolationism' that dominated domestic American politics in the inter-war years. Rather, it will likely lead- is already leading- to a keen debate about the precise role and limits of American power: and about the relationship between 'hard' power, including military power projection around the world, and 'soft' power, and, more broadly, and more importantly, to some kind of reassessment of America's strategic interests around the world.

No-one can be sure what, in detail, any such review or reassessment may entail. But the change in the American power position, as part of the emergence of a multi-polar world system, will be utterly crucial for Europe and its nascent foreign and security policy. In one sense, the character of the American-European relationship has always been the key to Europe's role in the world. During the Cold War era western Europe rested under the US nuclear umbrella accepted US leadership in the alliance. Then, after the collapse of the Soviet Union, Europe still relied upon US leadership in the first gulf war and then, embarrassingly, in Europe's own back yard during the Kosovo crisis. Also, after 9/11- a full decade since the end of the Cold War- Europe remained divided, this time by an assertive and unilateralist US policy in the Middle East. During the invasion of Iraq these divisions sharpened, with France and Germany on one side and Britain, Italy, Spain and most new member states on the other.

Now, though, in 2006, Europe is faced with a new world in which American power has obvious limits. These limits have created a geo-political vacuum out of which a multipolar world is already clearly beginning to emerge. Although Europe's economic strength marks her out, alongside the United States, China and India as one of the key 'poles' in the new global architecture, the EU can only reach her potential by a further burst of integration.

At the beginning of the 1990's the Maastricht treaty enshrined a 'Common Foreign and Security Policy' as an objective of the Union; and some key steps have already been taken in creating a momentum towards such a common policy. The creation of the euro-zone itself was a major step giving the Union a strong single voice in key aspects of global financial and economic policy. The trade regime of the EU (with its majority voting and single trade commissioner) has shown how a common position can give Europe immense power in global affairs. In defence policy, the St. Malo agreement between Europe's two main security powers, Britain and France, the setting of the Petersberg tasks, the organisation of EU Battlegroups and their deployments around the world, have all contributed, if not to the creation of a imminent Pentagon-style defence system, then, at least to the beginnings of a 'European Security and Defence Policy'. And on the diplomatic front the 'troika' of Britain, France and Germany has played a key role in negotiations with Iran, and, militarily, Italy and France have taken an unprecedented role for Europe in the Middle East by sending troops as part of the UN's peace-keeping force in southern Lebanon.

Both the CFSP and the ESDP, however, remain weak institutionally – a weakness caused by the continued dominance of 'sovereign' member states in defence and foreign policy. This weakness will continue until majority voting becomes the norm in common foreign and security policy matters. However, the EU has at least created a serious institutional framework around the High Representative's office of Javier Solana and the Policy Planning and Early Warning Unit, which act as a co-ordination centre for the Union's efforts. Solana's office is now well-established, is respected around the world, and works well with the Presidency. It can, at any time, be built upon and strengthened should the Union decide to do so.

Of course, great moves forward in institutional reform and integration in Europe tend to be dependent upon political will: and political is, inevitably, driven by events, and by the dynamic of global change. We are now, though, arguably, in such an era of change.

However, although there are real signs of such a growing political will behind Europe acting together in the world, such a new enthusiasm may not, in the first instance, declare itself exclusively through the Union's mechanisms- but rather emerge through increased operational co-operation between leading member states. We have already seen such co-operation and co-ordination in the European 'troika's' diplomacy in the negotiations over nuclear policy with Iran. The US-Iranian confrontation over Iran's nuclear policy has led to a unique co-ordination of British, French and German policy that amounts to a single European position. Also, the diplomatic and military co-ordination, through the UN, of France and Italy in helping to stabilise southern Lebanon, can rightly be seen as yet another example of an emerging European foreign and security policy. Although these co-operative actions by leading EU member states are not, strictly, formal EU initiatives, the EU, primarily in the form of Solana's office, has acted as driver and facilitator, and there can be little doubt that such co-operation amongst Europe's big actors- certainly should the initiatives produce some modicum of success- will create a greater sense of common purpose for the EU as a whole.

In this new era of European diplomatic and military co-operation Britain's role remains pivotal. The UK is a nuclear power, it spends more on defence than any other member state, and, intriguingly, its public opinion, whilst cool on Britain joining the euro-zone, is traditionally less hostile to the creation of a European Defence System. Yet, whilst Britain remains on the European sidelines, and still somewhat hesitant about developing a really serious CFSP or ESDP, a European foreign and security policy worthy of a superpower will simply not be achievable. In this sense the estrangement of Britain from 'core Europe' over the invasion of Iraq was a real set-back for Europe. But, post Iraq, Britain may well be reverting to its earlier, mid-1990's, approach when, following the European failure in the Balkans, Downing Street, through the St. Malo process, attempted to engage with other security powers in Europe to develop a more common European policy. As well as a possible shift in Britain's position, we may now be witnessing, following its clear set-back in Iraq, a change in Washington. As in the Clinton era, Washington may already be more accommodating to European defence and security integration, and to Britain's role in it. Washington cannot be expected, as it did in the past, to facilitate European integration, but it may not block it either.

As the leading powers in Europe increasingly work together on major geo-political issues then, inevitably, a common European identity of interest will grow. As will a growing understanding amongst Europeans of the common threats emanating from the dangerous world we inhabit- common threats posed by the environment, by migration, by terrorism, and by vulnerable energy supplies amongst others. In such an environment the idea that individual European nation-states can protect themselves outside of a European security environment will become fanciful, if not laughable.

Also, Europeans will need to adjust to the reality of a world in which they have common interests which are sometimes separate from the interests of other big powers such as the USA and China. It is the beginning of wisdom to understand that Europe can retain a strong over-arching alliance with the USA whilst, at the same time, taking a different position on some strategic questions. For instance, Europe already has what amounts to a 'common view' of the Arab-Israeli issue, a common policy which is shared by Britain, France, Germany and most other EU member states. This policy- of an 'even handed approach' which could lead to an honest broker position – is not one which the United States, even if it could agree to it, could aspire to. Also, Europe has a 'common view' – or virtually a 'common view' – of the need for a strategic energy relationship with energy-rich Russia, another European policy which the US might not support but which Europe needs to pursue. In the coming multi-polar world these and other European common interests should lead to a common position that, once established, can always be negotiated with the USA; such a negotiation is far healthier, and more realistic, than the recent relationship in which the USA was able to govern the West by playing-off European powers against each other, leaving Europe without a policy.

So, we may well be entering an era in which that elusive European political commitment will grow to the point where Europe's domestic politicians will begin to take institutional change seriously again. Whatever happens to the stalled European constitution, the proposals for streamlining the EU's decision-making in foreign and security policy remain essential. The creation of an EU Foreign Minister backed up by a foreign policy apparatus, including an external action service, becomes a minimum necessity- and, as earlier argued, the office of the existing office of the High Representative provides an existing platform. In the medium-term, however, these particular institutional changes will not, of themselves, serve to create the necessary unity and 'single voice' needed for a viable foreign policy for a superpower. Rather, a viable foreign policy for a superpower will only begin to emerge once the Union has decided to expand qualified majority voting on foreign and security questions. Such a radical departure may yet, though, be some time off. However, the EU could, as a start, decide to use and target its undoubted economic, financial and trading power in the world by adopting majority voting on decisions involving economic sanctions.

Also, the EU could push forward with another idea proposed in the stalled constitution- the notion of 'structured co-operation' in the defence field in which those European states willing to move ahead by co-operating and integrating more deeply should be free to do so.

European power in the world, however, rests on more than a streamlined EU decision-making process. Europe already has immense 'soft power', and, through its stable, democratic societies, acts as an attractive exemplar around the world. The carrot of European membership acts as a foreign policy tool to those neighbouring states who want to join or who may, one day, be in a position to join.

But Europe also needs 'hard power' instruments in order to achieve some of its objectives. One such should, indeed, be the ability to use, and to threaten to use, targeted economic sanctions to exert leverage. Also, the issue of 'hard' military power needs to be addressed. There is little support in Europe for the creation of a Pentagon-style military complex, or for Pentagon-style military spending. But the if the EU is going to continue to play a role in the forward deployment of its forces- whether in Battlegroups or in a more substantial rapid reaction force- the EU nations will need to start lessening the spending gap that now exists between the British and French on the one hand and most of the others, including Germany. In an age of global terrorism and instability any half-way serious European security policy needs increased real resources allocated to intelligence and technology. Part of it can come from the long-overdue erosion of wasteful duplication of intelligence and military hardware, and greater co-ordination of security resources by Brussels. But part must also come from increased spending, a real challenge for those European member states who, though clearly seeking the protection of a European-wide security policy, still harbour traditional resistance to defence spending.

There is also the thorny, and secretive, issue of Europe's nuclear weapons. The coming British decision on replacing its nuclear deterrent, the Trident system, with an up-dated version, or with none at all, represents a real opportunity for Europe. Realistically, Britain is not going to give up her nuclear weapons. So, one option is for Britain to go down the route of an expensive American replacement that retains an American hold over the British system; whereas the other is to buy the replacement from France, at a much lower cost, and to open the way for a truly European solution.

Finally, as Europe begins the slow, but definite, road towards a European foreign and security policy it is important to remember that the key characteristic of such a policy, and the key sign of Europe's arrival as a global power, is not the adoption of any particular policy: rather it is the unity deriving from the adoption of a common position. Such a common policy can be interventionist – as it tends to be at the moment in the Middle East, Africa, and Afghanistan. Or it can be quietist: staying out of these conflicts. But it is a common policy- which every member state has had a chance to participate in, and, once the decision is taken, every member state gets behind – that will bring Europe strength, purpose and influence. As things stand in 2006 the European Union is some way from securing the unified policy that marks out a global power. But the signs are that the next decade will see significant advances.

Conclusions and Recommendations

It has often been observed that the European Constitutional Treaty was in many respects primarily a codification and reordering of existing elements within the Treaty of Rome and its successor documents. Ironically, it now seems that rejection of the new Treaty in the French and Dutch referendums of 2005 was at least in part based upon hostility by the voters to provisions of its text which had already been in force for decades.

This last observation, however, is doubly inapplicable to the Constitutional Treaty's proposals in the field of external relations. The Treaty contained much that was new in this field and very few Dutch or French voters seem to have rejected the Constitution because of these novelties. Among the governments of the member states, the Treaty's provisions in the field of CFSP particularly represented something very like a discrete consensus, with no individual member state needing to be "compensated" for an unwelcome outcome in this field by counter-concessions in another chapter of the Treaty.

All these factors suggest that even if in the medium term it proves impossible to resurrect the Constitutional Treaty as whole, it may well be possible in the foreseeable future for the Union's member states to agree among themselves without undue difficulty a package of measures incorporating much of what was agreed under the Constitutional Treaty in the sphere of the Union's external relations. For both political and legal reasons (the latter depending upon the precise terms of the final agreement) it is likely that any such package would require at least some Treaty amendment, but this could easily be done by a limited number of changes to existing Treaty texts, reinforced if necessary by an Interinstitutional Agreement. These changes would probably not need to be ratified by referendums in most member states. Where a referendum was necessary, it would be an infinitely easier consultation for the government to win than that concerning the wide-ranging and studiedly ambiguous Constitutional Treaty. Opinion polls throughout the Union (including in the UK) strongly suggest that a more coherent and reinforced role for the Union on the world stage is a popular rather than controversial goal for national electorates. To meet French and other sensibilities, it might be necessary to exclude from the package some provisions relating to the Common Commercial Policy, but a European Foreign Minister, a European External Action Service, a stronger projection of soft power, and a genuine debate about "structured co-operation" in ESDP all seem realistically achievable goals by the end of the decade. It is on the basis of these achievable goals in the short and medium term that more ambitious changes in the longer term can and should be pursued.

Given the relatively favourable conjunction of circumstances surrounding development of the CFSP and the ESDP, it may seem strange that the incoming German Presidency apparently attaches such importance, as do a number of other member states, to attempts to revive the Constitutional Treaty in its entirety, rather than to sectoral achievement of its most significant provisions. The time and effort devoted to securing agreement on the Constitutional Treaty of 2004 will naturally make its most enthusiastic supporters reluctant to see it abandoned. But the danger must exist that continued insistence on the perhaps impossible eventual adoption of a revised Constitutional Treaty will simply prevent progress in specific areas where the Treaty sketched out a new, realistic and significant approach to challenging questions about the Union's future.

The authors of this report believe that the heads of state and government should already be considering alternative ways of improving the Union's CFSP and ESDP which do not depend upon the adoption of an overall European Constitutional Treaty. These improvements should be based upon the relevant provisions of the European Constitutional Treaty and which played little or no part in the Treaty's rejection by the French and Dutch electorates. Attempts to revive that Treaty in its entirety must either rapidly show real prospects for success, or they must be abandoned. Their unsuccessful prolongation would not merely be futile, but obstructive of other, more promising strategies.

It is worth pointing out in conclusion that the predominantly intergovernmental nature of CFSP and ESDP inevitably creates possibilities of "European" action which will proceed outside or only tenuously related to the Union's formal treaty structure. The negotiations of the French, British and German governments with Iran were a clear example of this phenomenon, giving rise to understandable fears of a European "Directoire" of the member states traditionally most active in global external policy. The St. Malo agreement was itself originally an agreement only between two countries, which has tentatively extended its reach to other members of the Union. Unless and until the member states, particularly the larger member states, are willing to move further down the road of the "Community method," notably as regards majority voting, such occasional initiatives in the broad sphere of external relations are probably, in the view of the authors, positive and healthy developments. They may in due course lead to the institutional consolidation of the Union's external policy which we would regard as the distant but nevertheless desirable goal. If the formation of a "Directoire" were the consequence of enhanced exchanges and co-ordination between the Union's leading actors on the external stage, then we would see that as a useful staging post on the route to a genuine common foreign and security policy for the Union. For Europe's partners in the world, it is not the precise internal structure of the EU's decision-making which counts, but rather its external impact.

Even bilateral initiatives within the Union have the capacity to play a role in this regard. Ernest Bevin famously wanted British nuclear weapons to have the "bloody Union Jack painted on them." If France and the United Kingdom could ever agree to develop a shared nuclear deterrent, it would not be necessary to paint the twelve stars on the delivery vehicle to emphasise its significance as a European military project. It is often remarked that such extra-European powers as China and India see Europe as more of a politically united entity than do many Europeans. An Anglo-French nuclear deterrent would not merely enhance the European Union's military credibility in the world. It would also enhance the Union's ability to contribute to global stability and security in fields going beyond the strictly military. The way in which the United States of America has in recent years exercised its "hard power" has overshadowed and diminished its ability to exercise its very considerable potential "soft power." There is no reason why the European Union should suffer the same fate if it develops its specifically military capacities over the coming decade. Throughout the Cold War, the United States was able to develop its resources of "hard" and "soft power" in parallel. That is the example that the European Union will be looking to emulate rather than the counterproductive American model of the past five years.

References

1   Treaty on the European Union, Title V, Art.J.1 para 2,
    Maastricht, 07.02.1992, p.7,
    www.eurotreaties.com/maastrichteu.pdf   [11.11.2006].

2   Amsterdam Treaty, Art.J.16, Amsterdam, 02.10.1997,
    p.13, http://www.eurotreaties.com/amsterdamtreaty.pdf
    [11.11.2006].

3   Working Group VII – ‚External Action', 'Final Report of
    Working Group VII on External Action', CONV 459/02,
    Brussels, 16.12.2002, pp.19-23, http://register.consilium.
    eu.int/pdf/en/02/cv00/00459en2.pdf [11.11.2006].

4   Contribution by Mr Dominique de Villepin and Mr
    Joschka Fischer, members of the Convention:
    'Contribution franco-allemande à la Convention
    européenne sur l'architecture institutionnelle de
    l'Union', CONV 489/03, Brussels, 16.01.2003,
    www.european-convention.eu.int [11.11.2006].

5   A Constitution for Europe, Part I Title V Chapter I
    http://europa.eu.int/constitution/en/ptoc5_en.htm#a25
    [11.11.2006].

6   International Spectator, Vol XL, No.1 Jan-Mar 2005; 'The
    EU Foreign Minister: Beyond Double-Hatting'

7   A Constitution for Europe http://europa.eu.int/
    constitution/en/allinone_en.htm [11.11.2006].

8   Consolidated Version of the Treaty on European Union,
    Art.18.1 and Art.18.2, 24.12.2002, pp.18-21,
    http://europa.eu.int/eur-lex/lex/en/treaties/dat/12002M/
    pdf/12002M_EN.pdf [11.11.2006].

9   Consolidated Version of the Treaty establishing the
    European Community, Art.213.2, 24.12.2002, p.88,
    http://europa.eu.int/eur-lex/lex/en/treaties/dat/
    12002E/pdf/12002E_EN.pdf [11.11.2006].

10 Proposal by Mr Giuliano Amato, Mr Elmar Brok and
    Mr Andrew Duff to the European Convention, Option 2:
    Declaration on the Creation of a European External
    Action Service, http://europeanconvention.eu.int/Docs/
    Treaty/pdf/873/Art%20III%20225a%20Amato%20EN.pdf
    [14.05.2006].

11 Constitutional Treaty, Part III Art.III-296 para3,
    http://europa.eu.int/constitution/en/ptoc66_en.htm
    [14.05.2006].

12 Brussels European Council – Presidency Conclusion,
    16/17.12 2004, p.23, http://ue.eu.int/ueDocs/cms_Data/
    docs/pressData/en/ec/83201.pdf [14.05.2006].

13 European Parliament resolution on the institutional
    aspects of the European External Action Service,
    26.05.2005, http://www.europarl.eu.int/omk/sipade3?L=
    en&objid=96093&mode=sip&nav=x&lstdoc=n&level=2
    [14.05.2006].

14 European External Action Service: Joint Progress
    Report to the European Council by the Secretary-
    General/High Representative and the Commission,
    Brussels, 09.06.2005.

15 European External Action Service: Joint Progress
    Report to the European Council by the Secretary-
    General/High Representative and the Commission,
    Brussels, 09.06.2005.

16 Allen, David (2004), 'So who will speak for Europe? The Constitutional Treaty and coherence in EU external relations', CFSP Forum, vol.2, issue 5, p.3, www.fornet.info [11.11.2006].

17 Solana, Javier (2000): The EU's external projection: improving the efficiency of our collective Resources, Brussels, p.11, http://ue.eu.int/ueDocs/cms_Data/docs/ pressdata/EN/reports/76748.pdf [11.11.2006].

18 Treaty of Nice, Declaration on Article 10 of the Treaty establishing the European Community, http://europa.eu.int/eur-lex/lex/en/treaties/dat/ 12001C/pdf/12001C_EN.pdf [11.11.2006].

19 Treaty on the European Union, Title V, Art.J.4 para 1, Maastricht, 07.02.1992, p.8, www.eurotreaties.com/maastrichteu.pdf [11.11.2006].

20 General Affairs Council Meeting, 'Statement on Improving Military Capabilities', Brussels, 9/20.11.2002.

21 General Affairs and External Relations Council, 'ESDP Presidency Report 2003', 09.12.2003, p.4, http://ue.eu.int/ueDocs/cms_Data/docs/ pressdata/en/misc/78343.pdf [11.11.2006].

22 Headline Goal 2010, p.2, http://ue.eu.int/uedocs/cmsUpload/ 2010%20Headline%20Goal.pdf [11.11.2006].

23 The Battlegroup concept – UK/France/Germany food for thought paper, http://ue.eu.int/uedocs/cmsUpload/ Battlegroups.pdf [11.11.2006].

24 Schmitt, Burkard (2005); ‚Defence Expenditure',
   Institute for Security Studies, p.3,
   http://www.iss-eu.org/esdp/11-bsdef.pdf
   [11.11.2006].

25 European Security Strategy, ‚A Secure Europe in a
   Better World', Brussels, 12.12.2003,
   http://ue.eu.int/uedocs/cmsUpload/78367.pdf
   [11.11.2006].

26 Brussels European Council, ‚Presidency Conclusion',
   16/16.12.2004, p.20, http://ue.eu.int/ueDocs/cms_Data/
   docs/pressData/en/ec/83201.pdf [11.11.2006].

27 General Affairs and External Relations Council, '
   'ESDP Presidency Report 2005', Brussels, 19.12.2005,
   http://register.consilium.eu.int/pdf/en/05/st15/
   st15891.en05.pdf [11.11.2006].

28 Consolidated Version of the Treaty on the European
   Union, Art.28,
   http://europa.eu.int/eur-lex/lex/en/treaties/dat/
   12002M/htm/C_2002325EN.000501.html [11.11.2006].

29 Draft Treaty establishing a Constitution for Europe,
   Brussels, 18.07.2003, http://european-convention.eu.int/
   docs/Treaty/cv00850.en03.pdf [11.11.2006].

30 Constitutional Treaty, Part III, Title V, Chapter III,
   http://europa.eu/constitution/en/ptoc69_e n.htm#a397
   [11.11.2006].

Acknowledgement

We would like thank the James Madison Trust for its financial support for the research project leading to this report.